The History

The Heart of Scandinavia

Copyright © 2023 by Gustav-David Nilsson and Einar Felix Hansen.

All rights reserved. No part of this publication may be reproduced, stored in a retrieval system, or transmitted, in any form or by any means, electronic, mechanical, photocopying, recording, or otherwise, without the prior written permission of the copyright holder. This book was created with the help of Artificial Intelligence technology.

The contents of this book are intended for entertainment purposes only. While every effort has been made to ensure the accuracy and reliability of the information presented, the author and publisher make no warranties or representations as to the accuracy, completeness, or suitability of the information contained herein. The information presented in this book is not intended as a substitute for professional advice, and readers should consult with qualified professionals in the relevant fields for specific advice.

Introduction to Sweden and its geography 6

Prehistoric Sweden: Stone Age and Bronze Age 8

Iron Age and Migration Period 10

Vikings and the Age of Expansion 12

The Christianization of Sweden 14

The Rise of the Kalmar Union 16

The Era of Gustav Vasa 18

The Power Struggle of the Vasa Dynasty 20

The Thirty Years' War and Sweden's Great Power Era 23

Queen Christina and the Enlightenment 26

The Age of Freedom 28

The Napoleonic Wars and Sweden's Reconciliation with Russia 30

Industrialization and Urbanization 32

The Union between Sweden and Norway 34

The Emergence of Social Democracy 36

Sweden's Neutrality in World War I 38

The Interwar Period and the Rise of Fascism 40

Sweden in World War II 42

The Post-War Social Democratic Consensus 44

The Swedish Model of Welfare 46

The 1968 Movement and its Impact on Swedish Society 48

Sweden's Foreign Policy during the Cold War 50

The Assassination of Olof Palme 52

Sweden in the European Union 54

Contemporary Politics and Society 56

Swedish Art and Culture 58

Conclusion and Reflections on Sweden's History 60

Introduction to Sweden and its geography

Sweden is a Scandinavian country located in Northern Europe. It is the third largest country in the European Union, with a population of over 10 million people. The country shares borders with Norway to the west, Finland to the northeast, and is connected to Denmark by a bridge-tunnel across the Øresund Strait to the south.

Sweden has a diverse geography that includes mountains, forests, lakes, and a long coastline. Its landscape is dominated by the Scandinavian Mountains, which run from north to south along the western border of the country. The highest peak, Kebnekaise, stands at 2,111 meters (6,926 ft) above sea level. The mountain range is home to some of Sweden's most popular ski resorts and hiking trails.

The eastern part of Sweden is characterized by lowlands and forests. The country's largest lake, Vänern, is located in this area, and the Göta Canal, a 190 km long canal that stretches from Gothenburg on the west coast to Söderköping on the east coast, connects it to the Baltic Sea. The canal is a popular tourist attraction, and boat trips are available during the summer months.

The Swedish coastline is over 3,200 km long and is dotted with islands, archipelagos, and fjords. The Stockholm archipelago, located in the Baltic Sea, consists of over 30,000 islands and islets, making it one of the largest archipelagos in the world. The archipelago is a popular destination for sailing, kayaking, and fishing.

Sweden has a temperate climate, with four distinct seasons. The summer months, from June to August, are usually mild and pleasant, with temperatures averaging between 20°C and 25°C (68°F and 77°F). The winter months, from December to February, are cold and snowy, with temperatures averaging between -4°C and -10°C (25°F and 14°F). The northern part of the country experiences polar nights in the winter, with no sunlight for several weeks, and midnight sun in the summer, with daylight for 24 hours.

Sweden is a constitutional monarchy with a parliamentary system of government. The monarch is the head of state, but holds no political power. The country is divided into 21 counties, which are further divided into municipalities. Stockholm is the capital city of Sweden, and is also the largest city in the country, with a population of over 1.3 million people. Other major cities include Gothenburg, Malmö, Uppsala, and Linköping.

In conclusion, Sweden is a country with a diverse geography, a temperate climate, and a rich history and culture. Its landscape includes mountains, forests, lakes, and a long coastline, offering a wide range of outdoor activities and attractions for visitors. With a constitutional monarchy and a parliamentary system of government, Sweden is a stable and prosperous country that values equality, human rights, and environmental sustainability.

Prehistoric Sweden: Stone Age and Bronze Age

The prehistoric period in Sweden, which dates back to approximately 10,000 BCE, is characterized by the use of stone tools and weapons. During this time, the climate was much colder than it is today, and large parts of Sweden were covered by ice. As the climate warmed and the ice retreated, humans gradually migrated into the region.

The earliest evidence of human habitation in Sweden comes from the Maglemosian culture, which existed from around 9,000 to 6,000 BCE. This culture was characterized by the use of microliths, small stone tools that were used in hunting and fishing.

Around 6,000 BCE, a new culture known as the Kongemose culture emerged in Denmark and southern Sweden. This culture was characterized by the use of large, bifacial stone tools and the development of agriculture and animal husbandry. Over time, the Kongemose culture spread northwards into Sweden, and by around 4,000 BCE, had evolved into the Ertebølle culture, which was focused on fishing and shellfish gathering.

Around 2,500 BCE, a new culture known as the Battle Axe culture emerged in southern Scandinavia. This culture was characterized by the use of polished stone battle axes and the development of copper and bronze metallurgy. The Battle Axe culture spread northwards into Sweden, where it evolved into the Nordic Bronze Age.

The Nordic Bronze Age, which lasted from approximately 1,800 to 500 BCE, was a period of significant social and cultural change in Sweden. During this time, metalworking became widespread, and bronze tools and weapons replaced stone ones. The society became more hierarchical, with a ruling class that controlled trade and the distribution of goods. The period also saw the construction of large burial mounds and other monumental structures, indicating a growing sense of social and cultural identity.

The Nordic Bronze Age saw the emergence of several distinct regional cultures in Sweden, each with its own unique traditions and practices. In the southern part of the country, the cultures were strongly influenced by the Germanic peoples to the south, while in the northern part, the cultures were more closely related to those of Finland and the Baltic States.

In conclusion, the prehistoric period in Sweden, which spans from approximately 10,000 BCE to 500 BCE, was a time of significant change and development. The early Stone Age saw the use of microliths for hunting and fishing, while the Bronze Age saw the development of metalworking and the emergence of distinct regional cultures. These early periods laid the foundation for the later developments in Swedish society and culture.

Iron Age and Migration Period

The Iron Age in Sweden lasted from approximately 500 BCE to 800 CE and was characterized by the widespread use of iron tools and weapons. This period saw significant cultural and social changes, as well as the arrival of new peoples and cultures from outside of Scandinavia.

During the early Iron Age, Swedish society was organized into small, decentralized communities. These communities were typically led by chieftains who were responsible for maintaining social order and resolving disputes. Agriculture and animal husbandry were the primary means of subsistence, and long-distance trade networks began to emerge, connecting Sweden with other parts of Europe.

In the 1st century CE, the Roman historian Tacitus wrote about the Germanic tribes that inhabited Scandinavia, including the Suiones, who were believed to be the ancestors of the modern-day Swedes. The Suiones were described as a powerful people who controlled a large territory that included much of modern-day Sweden.

During the Migration Period, which lasted from approximately 400 to 800 CE, new peoples and cultures began to arrive in Sweden from outside of Scandinavia. The Goths, who were originally from modern-day Poland and Ukraine, settled in southern Sweden, while the Sarmatians, who were from modern-day Russia, settled in the north.

The Migration Period also saw the emergence of several powerful kingdoms in Sweden, including the Geats in the south and the Swedes in the north. These kingdoms were characterized by complex social hierarchies and powerful warrior elites. The period also saw the development of a system of runic writing, which was used for both practical and religious purposes.

The arrival of Christianity in Sweden is thought to have occurred during the Migration Period, with the earliest known Christian artifacts dating back to the 6th century CE. However, it was not until the 11th century CE that Christianity became the dominant religion in Sweden.

In conclusion, the Iron Age and Migration Period in Sweden were characterized by significant cultural and social changes, as well as the arrival of new peoples and cultures from outside of Scandinavia. The emergence of powerful kingdoms and the development of a system of runic writing laid the foundation for the later developments in Swedish society and culture.

Vikings and the Age of Expansion

The Viking Age in Sweden lasted from approximately 800 to 1050 CE and was characterized by the widespread expansion and exploration of the Vikings, who were seafaring warriors and traders from Scandinavia. During this period, Swedish Vikings, also known as Varangians, played a significant role in the expansion of the Viking Empire, which stretched from the Baltic Sea to North America.

The Vikings were known for their seafaring skills and their longships, which were designed for speed and maneuverability. They used these ships to travel across the seas and rivers of Europe, trading goods and engaging in raiding and pillaging. The Viking expansion brought them into contact with a wide range of cultures and peoples, including the Franks, the Slavs, and the Byzantine Empire.

The Vikings from Sweden, known as Varangians, were particularly skilled in sailing on the rivers of Eastern Europe and the Black Sea. They established trade routes along the Volga River and formed alliances with local rulers, often serving as mercenaries in their armies. The Varangians also established settlements in the region, including the city of Novgorod, which became an important center of trade and commerce.

The Viking Age also saw the emergence of powerful kingdoms in Sweden, including the Svear and the Götar. These kingdoms were characterized by a highly stratified social hierarchy, with powerful warrior elites at the top and farmers and artisans at the bottom. The Viking expansion brought wealth and power to these elites, who used it to build impressive fortresses and monuments, such as the famous Viking burial mounds.

During the later part of the Viking Age, Sweden became increasingly involved in the politics of the wider Viking world. The 11th century saw the emergence of a powerful Swedish dynasty, the House of Stenkil, which sought to expand Sweden's influence and power. The dynasty established close ties with the Danish and Norwegian monarchies and sought to establish a unified Scandinavian kingdom.

In conclusion, the Viking Age in Sweden was a time of significant expansion and exploration, as the Vikings from Sweden, or Varangians, played a key role in the Viking Empire. The period saw the emergence of powerful kingdoms in Sweden and the construction of impressive fortresses and monuments. The later part of the Viking Age saw Sweden becoming increasingly involved in the politics of the wider Viking world, as the House of Stenkil sought to expand Sweden's influence and power.

The Christianization of Sweden

The Christianization of Sweden was a gradual process that began in the 9th century CE and was not completed until the 12th century CE. During this period, Christianity gradually replaced the traditional pagan religions that had been practiced in Sweden for centuries.

The first recorded instance of Christianity in Sweden dates back to the 9th century CE, when a monk named Ansgar visited the court of King Bjorn of Sweden. Ansgar was a missionary from the Carolingian Empire, and he was attempting to spread Christianity throughout Scandinavia. Although King Bjorn was not converted, Ansgar was allowed to establish a Christian presence in Sweden.

In the 11th century CE, the powerful Danish king, Canute the Great, invaded Sweden and attempted to impose Christianity on the Swedish people. Although Canute was not successful in converting Sweden, his invasion brought the Christian faith to the attention of the Swedish ruling class, who saw the benefits of adopting Christianity, including trade relations with Christian Europe and the potential for political alliances.

The first official Christian king of Sweden was Inge the Elder, who ruled from 1079 to 1105 CE. Inge was initially a pagan, but he converted to Christianity after his brother was killed in a pagan uprising. Inge then began a campaign to convert his subjects to Christianity, and he was supported in this effort by the Archbishop of Bremen, who established a mission in Sweden.

The conversion of the Swedish people to Christianity was a slow and gradual process, and it was not completed until the 12th century CE. One of the most significant events in the Christianization of Sweden was the establishment of the Swedish Church in 1164 CE. The Swedish Church was initially under the control of the Archbishop of Lund, but it later became independent, with its own archbishop based in Uppsala.

The Christianization of Sweden had a significant impact on Swedish society and culture. Christianity brought with it new ideas about morality and social order, as well as a new system of education and literacy. The church became a powerful force in Swedish society, and it played a key role in the political and cultural development of the country.

In conclusion, the Christianization of Sweden was a gradual process that began in the 9th century CE and was not completed until the 12th century CE. Christianity brought with it new ideas about morality and social order, and it had a significant impact on Swedish society and culture. The church became a powerful force in Swedish society, and it played a key role in the political and cultural development of the country.

The Rise of the Kalmar Union

The Kalmar Union was a political union between Denmark, Norway, and Sweden that was established in 1397 CE. The union was named after the city of Kalmar in southern Sweden, where the treaty establishing the union was signed.

The Kalmar Union was the result of political and economic pressures that were affecting the three Scandinavian countries at the time. Denmark, Norway, and Sweden had all been struggling to assert their independence and to maintain their own political and economic power. The union was seen as a way to unify the three countries and to create a more powerful and stable political entity.

The union was led by a monarch, who was chosen from among the ruling families of Denmark, Norway, and Sweden. The first monarch of the union was Queen Margaret I of Denmark, who had been ruling over Denmark and Norway since 1375 CE. Margaret was a skilled diplomat and politician, and she was able to negotiate the terms of the union with the ruling families of Norway and Sweden.

Under the terms of the union, Denmark, Norway, and Sweden would retain their own laws, languages, and customs, but they would be governed by a common monarch and a common council. The council was responsible for the administration of the union, including foreign affairs, trade, and defense.

The Kalmar Union was a significant political and economic power in Europe during the 15th century. The union controlled the trade routes between the Baltic Sea and the North Sea, and it had a strong navy that was able to protect its interests in the region. The union also played a key role in the development of the Hanseatic League, a powerful trading organization that controlled much of the trade in northern Europe.

The Kalmar Union was not without its challenges, however. The union was often beset by internal conflicts and rivalries, particularly between Denmark and Sweden. The union also faced external pressures, including threats from powerful neighbors such as the Hanseatic League and the German Empire.

The Kalmar Union officially came to an end in 1523, when Gustav Vasa became king of Sweden and led a rebellion against the union. The rebellion was successful, and Sweden became an independent kingdom once again.

In conclusion, the Kalmar Union was a significant political and economic power in Europe during the 15th century. The union was established as a way to unify Denmark, Norway, and Sweden and to create a more powerful and stable political entity. Although the union faced significant challenges and ultimately came to an end, it played a key role in the development of Scandinavian politics and culture.

The Era of Gustav Vasa

Gustav Vasa was a Swedish nobleman who played a pivotal role in the history of Sweden during the 16th century. Gustav Vasa was born in 1496, and he became the king of Sweden in 1523, after leading a successful rebellion against the Kalmar Union.

Gustav Vasa's reign was characterized by significant political and social changes. He established a strong central government in Sweden and worked to modernize the country's economy and infrastructure. He also played a key role in the establishment of the Swedish Lutheran Church, which became the dominant religion in Sweden.

One of Gustav Vasa's most significant achievements was his efforts to reform the Swedish economy. He encouraged the development of mining and manufacturing, and he established a national currency to replace the patchwork of local currencies that had been in use in Sweden. Gustav Vasa also worked to improve transportation and communication in Sweden, building roads and bridges and establishing a postal service.

Gustav Vasa's reign also saw significant changes in Swedish politics. He established a strong central government in Stockholm and worked to strengthen the power of the monarchy. He also introduced new laws and regulations that helped to modernize Swedish society and to create a more stable and orderly political system.

Gustav Vasa was also a key figure in the Protestant Reformation in Sweden. He embraced the ideas of Martin

Luther and worked to establish the Swedish Lutheran Church as the official religion of Sweden. Gustav Vasa also confiscated the wealth and property of the Catholic Church in Sweden, which helped to fund his reforms and modernization efforts.

Gustav Vasa's reign was not without its challenges, however. He faced significant opposition from powerful nobles who resented his centralization of power and his attempts to limit their influence. Gustav Vasa also faced threats from neighboring countries, including Denmark and Russia.

In conclusion, Gustav Vasa's reign was a significant period in the history of Sweden. His efforts to modernize the Swedish economy and infrastructure helped to create a more stable and prosperous society. His political reforms helped to establish a strong central government in Sweden, and his establishment of the Swedish Lutheran Church helped to shape the religious and cultural identity of Sweden for centuries to come. Despite facing significant challenges, Gustav Vasa's legacy continues to be felt in Sweden today.

The Power Struggle of the Vasa Dynasty

The Vasa Dynasty was one of the most important royal houses in Swedish history, and it played a significant role in shaping the political and cultural identity of Sweden. The dynasty was founded by Gustav Vasa, who became king of Sweden in 1523, and it continued to rule Sweden until the death of Charles XII in 1718.

The Vasa Dynasty was characterized by significant political and social changes, including the establishment of a strong central government, the expansion of Swedish territory, and the development of the Swedish economy and infrastructure. However, the dynasty was also marked by a power struggle between the monarchy and the nobility, as well as between rival factions within the monarchy itself.

The first few generations of the Vasa Dynasty were marked by relative stability and prosperity. Gustav Vasa's son, Erik XIV, was a capable ruler who expanded Sweden's territory and worked to establish a more efficient and effective government. However, Erik XIV's reign was also marked by a power struggle with his brothers, Johan and Karl, who eventually deposed him and took the throne for themselves.

The reign of Johan III, the son of Johan Vasa, was marked by significant religious and cultural changes. Johan III was a devout Catholic, and he worked to establish a more tolerant and diverse society in Sweden. He also encouraged the development of the arts and sciences, and he founded the University of Uppsala, which became a center of learning and scholarship in Sweden.

However, Johan III's reign was also marked by a power struggle with his brother, Duke Charles, who sought to limit the power of the monarchy and increase the influence of the nobility. This struggle eventually led to a civil war in Sweden, which was won by Johan III and his supporters.

The reign of Gustav II Adolph, the son of Johan III, was marked by significant military victories and the expansion of Swedish territory. Gustav II Adolph led Sweden to victory in the Thirty Years' War and established Sweden as a major European power. However, his reign was also marked by a power struggle with the Swedish nobility, who resented his centralization of power and his attempts to limit their influence.

The later part of the Vasa Dynasty was marked by increasing political instability and social unrest. The reign of Christina, the daughter of Gustav II Adolph, was marked by significant religious and cultural changes, but it was also marked by a power struggle between the monarchy and the nobility. This struggle eventually led to the abdication of Christina in 1654.

The reign of Charles XI, the son of Christina, was marked by significant efforts to strengthen the power of the monarchy and to limit the influence of the nobility. Charles XI centralized power in Stockholm and worked to establish a more efficient and effective government. However, his reign was also marked by a power struggle with the Swedish nobility, who resented his attempts to limit their influence.

In conclusion, the power struggle of the Vasa Dynasty was a significant period in the history of Sweden. The dynasty was characterized by significant political and social changes, including the establishment of a strong central government and the expansion of Swedish territory. However, the dynasty was also marked by a power struggle between the monarchy and the nobility, as well as between rival factions within the monarchy itself. Despite facing significant challenges, the Vasa Dynasty played a key role in shaping the political and cultural identity of Sweden for centuries to come.

The Thirty Years' War and Sweden's Great Power Era

The Thirty Years' War was one of the most significant conflicts in European history, and it played a pivotal role in shaping the political and military power of Sweden during the 17th century. The war was fought between 1618 and 1648, and it involved most of the major European powers, including Sweden.

Sweden's involvement in the Thirty Years' War was largely driven by the ambitions of King Gustav II Adolph, who saw an opportunity to expand Sweden's territory and influence in Europe. Gustav II Adolph saw the war as a chance to establish Sweden as a major European power and to challenge the dominance of the Holy Roman Empire.

Sweden entered the war in 1629, and Gustav II Adolph quickly established himself as a skilled military leader. He won a series of decisive battles in Germany and established Sweden as a major player in the conflict. Gustav II Adolph's military victories helped to cement Sweden's position as a Great Power in Europe and helped to establish the Swedish Empire.

However, Gustav II Adolph's ambitions came at a significant cost to Sweden. The war was expensive, and it drained Sweden's resources and manpower. Sweden was forced to raise taxes and to conscript soldiers to fight in the war, which led to significant social unrest and political instability.

Despite these challenges, Sweden continued to play a significant role in the Thirty Years' War, and Gustav II Adolph continued to win important victories in Germany. However, his luck eventually ran out, and he was killed in battle in 1632.

Following Gustav II Adolph's death, Sweden's involvement in the Thirty Years' War became more complicated. The country was ruled by Queen Christina, who was more interested in cultural and intellectual pursuits than in military conquests. Christina eventually abdicated in 1654, and she was succeeded by Charles X Gustav, who was more interested in military expansion and territorial conquests.

Under Charles X Gustav's leadership, Sweden continued to play a significant role in European politics and military affairs. Charles X Gustav led Sweden to victory in the Second Northern War, which saw Sweden expand its territory and establish control over large parts of the Baltic region.

However, Sweden's military successes came at a significant cost. The country was heavily in debt, and its resources and manpower were stretched thin. The Great Power era of Sweden was marked by significant social unrest and political instability, as well as by challenges from neighboring countries such as Russia and Denmark.

In conclusion, the Thirty Years' War played a significant role in Sweden's Great Power era. Sweden's involvement in the war helped to establish the country as a major European power, but it also came at a significant cost to Sweden's resources and manpower. The Great Power era of Sweden was marked by significant social unrest and political instability, and it was ultimately brought to an end by the country's inability to sustain its military and economic power.

Queen Christina and the Enlightenment

Queen Christina of Sweden was one of the most fascinating figures of the 17th century, and she played a significant role in the cultural and intellectual development of Sweden and Europe during the Enlightenment period. Christina was born in 1626 and was the daughter of King Gustav II Adolph, who had been killed in battle during the Thirty Years' War.

Christina became Queen of Sweden in 1632 at the age of six, following the death of her father. She was raised by her mother and a council of regents, who were responsible for governing the country in her stead until she came of age.

When Christina reached adulthood, she proved to be a remarkable and unconventional ruler. She was deeply interested in the arts and sciences, and she became a patron of many artists, writers, and philosophers. She also championed religious tolerance and freedom of thought, which were important tenets of the Enlightenment.

Christina's interests in art and culture led her to establish the famous Academy of Arcadia, which was a gathering place for intellectuals and artists in Rome. Christina also amassed a significant collection of art and books, which she eventually donated to the Vatican.

Despite her interest in culture and the arts, Christina's reign was not without its challenges. She faced significant opposition from the Swedish nobility, who resented her attempts to limit their power and influence. She was also criticized for her unconventional behavior, which included wearing men's clothing and behaving in a manner that was considered scandalous for a woman of her station.

In 1654, Christina shocked Europe by abdicating the throne and converting to Catholicism. She left Sweden and spent the remainder of her life traveling and pursuing her interests in art and culture.

Christina's impact on Sweden and Europe was significant. She helped to establish Sweden as a center of intellectual and cultural life during the Enlightenment, and she played a key role in promoting religious tolerance and freedom of thought. Her legacy continues to be felt in Sweden and Europe to this day.

In conclusion, Queen Christina of Sweden was a remarkable and unconventional ruler who played a significant role in the cultural and intellectual development of Sweden and Europe during the Enlightenment. Her interest in art and culture, as well as her commitment to religious tolerance and freedom of thought, helped to establish Sweden as a center of intellectual life during this period. Despite facing significant opposition and criticism, Christina's legacy continues to be celebrated and admired by scholars and cultural enthusiasts around the world.

The Age of Freedom

The Age of Freedom, also known as the Age of Liberty, was a significant period in Swedish history that lasted from 1718 to 1772. It was a time of significant political and social change, characterized by a shift towards democracy and the establishment of civil rights and freedoms for the Swedish people.

The Age of Freedom began with the death of Charles XII, the last king of the Vasa Dynasty, in 1718. The Swedish government was reorganized under a new system of government known as the Riksdag, which consisted of four estates: the nobility, the clergy, the burghers, and the peasants. This system of government marked a significant departure from the centralized monarchy of the Vasa Dynasty, and it gave more power to the people.

The Riksdag was responsible for making laws and governing the country, and it was characterized by a spirit of cooperation and compromise. This period was marked by significant social and economic changes, including the emergence of a strong middle class and the growth of industry and commerce.

During the Age of Freedom, Sweden became a center for the Enlightenment, which was a cultural and intellectual movement that emphasized reason, science, and individualism. This period saw the emergence of many important cultural and intellectual figures, including the philosopher Emanuel Swedenborg, the poet Carl Michael Bellman, and the scientist Carl Linnaeus.

The Age of Freedom was also marked by significant achievements in the field of education. The Swedish government invested heavily in education, and it established many new schools and universities, including the University of Uppsala and the Royal Swedish Academy of Sciences.

Despite these achievements, the Age of Freedom was not without its challenges. Sweden faced significant military and economic challenges, including a war with Russia and a financial crisis that threatened to undermine the country's stability.

The Age of Freedom came to an end in 1772, when Gustav III seized power in a bloodless coup. Gustav III sought to centralize power in the monarchy and limit the power of the Riksdag, marking a significant departure from the spirit of cooperation and compromise that had characterized the Age of Freedom.

In conclusion, the Age of Freedom was a significant period in Swedish history that was marked by a shift towards democracy and the establishment of civil rights and freedoms for the Swedish people. It was characterized by a spirit of cooperation and compromise, and it saw significant achievements in the fields of culture, education, and industry. Despite facing significant challenges, the Age of Freedom marked a turning point in Swedish history and helped to shape the country's political and cultural identity for centuries to come.

The Napoleonic Wars and Sweden's Reconciliation with Russia

The Napoleonic Wars were a series of conflicts that were fought between France and a coalition of European powers, including Russia and Sweden. The wars had a significant impact on Swedish history, and they marked a period of significant change and transformation for the country.

Sweden initially sided with Britain in the Napoleonic Wars, and the country played an important role in the war effort. Sweden joined the coalition against France in 1813, and the Swedish army fought in several important battles, including the Battle of Leipzig.

Despite their initial success, the coalition against France began to unravel as the war dragged on. In 1814, Sweden was forced to sign the Treaty of Kiel, which saw the country cede control of Norway to Denmark. The treaty was a significant blow to Swedish pride and power, and it marked a period of significant political and economic instability.

However, the Napoleonic Wars also marked the beginning of a period of reconciliation between Sweden and Russia. Sweden and Russia had been bitter rivals for centuries, but the two countries found themselves on the same side in the Napoleonic Wars. The cooperation between Sweden and Russia during the war marked the beginning of a period of improved relations between the two countries.

The improved relations between Sweden and Russia were further strengthened by the Treaty of Fredrikshamn, which was signed in 1809. The treaty saw Sweden cede control of Finland to Russia, but it also established a framework for cooperation and reconciliation between the two countries.

Despite the loss of Finland and the setbacks of the Napoleonic Wars, Sweden emerged from the conflict as a more united and stable country. The wars had brought about significant changes in Swedish society, including the growth of industry and commerce and the emergence of a strong middle class.

In conclusion, the Napoleonic Wars marked a period of significant change and transformation for Sweden. The country played an important role in the war effort, but it also suffered significant setbacks and losses. However, the wars also marked the beginning of a period of reconciliation between Sweden and Russia, and they helped to lay the foundation for improved relations between the two countries. The Napoleonic Wars marked a turning point in Swedish history, and they helped to shape the country's political and cultural identity for centuries to come.

Industrialization and Urbanization

The 19th century marked a period of significant change and transformation for Sweden, as the country underwent a process of industrialization and urbanization. The growth of industry and commerce had a significant impact on Swedish society, and it helped to shape the country's economic, political, and cultural identity for centuries to come.

The process of industrialization began in the mid-19th century, as Sweden embraced new technologies and methods of production. The country's natural resources, including iron ore and timber, were key to its industrial development, and they helped to establish Sweden as a center of manufacturing and trade.

The growth of industry led to significant social and economic changes, including the emergence of a strong middle class and the growth of urban areas. The cities of Stockholm, Gothenburg, and Malmö grew rapidly during this period, as people flocked to urban areas in search of work and opportunities.

The growth of urban areas led to significant changes in Swedish society. The cities became centers of culture and commerce, and they helped to shape the country's political and cultural identity. The emergence of a strong middle class also had a significant impact on Swedish society, as it helped to promote social mobility and economic opportunity for a broader range of people.

Despite the many benefits of industrialization and urbanization, the process was not without its challenges. The growth of industry led to significant environmental problems, including pollution and deforestation. The rapid growth of urban areas also led to significant social problems, including poverty, crime, and social unrest.

However, Sweden was able to overcome these challenges and emerge as a stronger and more prosperous country. The government invested heavily in infrastructure, including roads, railways, and public transportation, which helped to improve the quality of life for many Swedes.

In conclusion, the process of industrialization and urbanization had a significant impact on Swedish society and helped to shape the country's economic, political, and cultural identity. The growth of industry and commerce led to significant social and economic changes, including the emergence of a strong middle class and the growth of urban areas. Despite the many challenges that came with industrialization and urbanization, Sweden was able to overcome these obstacles and emerge as a prosperous and modern country.

The Union between Sweden and Norway

In 1814, Sweden and Norway were united under a single monarchy, in a union that would last for nearly a century. The union between Sweden and Norway was marked by significant political and cultural differences, as well as tensions between the two countries.

The union between Sweden and Norway was established in the aftermath of the Napoleonic Wars, as Sweden sought to consolidate its power in the region. Norway had previously been part of Denmark, but it was ceded to Sweden as part of the Treaty of Kiel.

The union was marked by significant political and cultural differences between the two countries. Sweden was a constitutional monarchy with a strong tradition of representative government, while Norway was an absolute monarchy with little political freedom. This led to significant tensions between the two countries, as Norway sought greater political autonomy within the union.

The tensions between Sweden and Norway came to a head in 1905, when Norway declared its independence from Sweden. The move was largely peaceful, and it was supported by a majority of the Norwegian population.

Despite the tensions between the two countries, the union between Sweden and Norway had significant benefits for both nations. The union helped to promote economic growth and cultural exchange, and it helped to establish Sweden and Norway as important players in the region.

The union also had a significant impact on Swedish identity, as it helped to shape the country's political and cultural identity for decades to come. The experience of the union helped to establish Sweden as a modern and progressive country, and it helped to promote democratic ideals and political freedom.

In conclusion, the union between Sweden and Norway was a significant period in Swedish history, marked by significant political and cultural differences between the two countries. Despite the tensions and challenges that came with the union, it helped to promote economic growth and cultural exchange, and it helped to establish Sweden and Norway as important players in the region. The union also had a significant impact on Swedish identity, helping to shape the country's political and cultural identity for decades to come.

The Emergence of Social Democracy

The emergence of social democracy was a significant period in Swedish history, as it helped to shape the country's political and social identity for decades to come. Social democracy emerged in Sweden in the early 20th century, and it was marked by a commitment to social justice, economic equality, and democratic participation.

The Swedish Social Democratic Party was founded in 1889, and it quickly became one of the most powerful political forces in the country. The party was committed to a range of progressive policies, including universal suffrage, public education, and social welfare programs.

Social democracy became particularly popular in Sweden in the aftermath of World War II, as the country sought to rebuild and modernize its economy. The Social Democratic Party won a majority in the 1946 general election, and it held power for much of the post-war period.

The Social Democratic Party introduced a range of progressive policies during this period, including the establishment of a comprehensive welfare state, which provided social insurance, healthcare, and education to all citizens. The party also implemented a range of economic policies designed to promote economic growth and improve living standards.

The emergence of social democracy had a significant impact on Swedish society, helping to promote economic equality and social justice. The country's commitment to social democracy helped to establish Sweden as a leader in the global progressive movement, and it helped to shape the country's political and cultural identity for decades to come.

Despite its many achievements, social democracy also faced significant challenges in Sweden. The growth of globalization and the rise of neoliberalism in the late 20th century led to significant economic and political changes, which challenged the country's commitment to social democracy. However, the legacy of social democracy remains a significant aspect of Swedish history and culture, and it continues to shape the country's political and social identity to this day.

In conclusion, the emergence of social democracy was a significant period in Swedish history, marked by a commitment to social justice, economic equality, and democratic participation. The Social Democratic Party played a key role in the development of social democracy in Sweden, introducing a range of progressive policies designed to promote economic growth and improve living standards. Despite its challenges, the legacy of social democracy remains an important aspect of Swedish history and culture, helping to shape the country's political and social identity for decades to come.

Sweden's Neutrality in World War I

Sweden's neutrality in World War I was a significant period in Swedish history, as the country sought to maintain its political and economic independence in the face of global conflict. Sweden's position of neutrality was based on a longstanding tradition of non-alignment and a commitment to peace.

When World War I broke out in 1914, Sweden declared its neutrality and sought to remain neutral throughout the conflict. The country's decision to remain neutral was based on a range of factors, including its economic interests, its strategic location, and its commitment to peace and diplomacy.

Sweden's neutrality was not without its challenges, however. The country was heavily dependent on trade with both the Allied and Central Powers, and it faced significant economic pressures as a result of the war. The country also faced challenges in terms of national security, as both sides sought to secure strategic advantages in the region.

Despite these challenges, Sweden was able to maintain its neutrality throughout the war, and it played an important role in international diplomacy and humanitarian efforts. Sweden was one of the few neutral countries to participate in the Hague Conventions, which sought to establish rules for the conduct of war and protect civilian populations.

Sweden's neutrality during World War I helped to establish the country as a leader in international diplomacy and humanitarian efforts. The country played an important role in the establishment of the League of Nations, which sought to promote peace and stability in the aftermath of the war.

In conclusion, Sweden's neutrality in World War I was a significant period in Swedish history, marked by a commitment to peace and diplomacy. Despite the challenges faced by the country, Sweden was able to maintain its neutrality throughout the conflict, and it played an important role in international diplomacy and humanitarian efforts. Sweden's position of neutrality helped to establish the country as a leader in international affairs and set the stage for its continued commitment to peace and diplomacy in the decades to come.

The Interwar Period and the Rise of Fascism

The interwar period was a turbulent time in Swedish history, marked by significant political and economic changes. The country faced a range of challenges during this period, including the rise of fascism in Europe and the global economic depression.

Sweden was able to avoid the worst effects of the global economic depression, largely due to the country's commitment to a range of social welfare programs and economic policies designed to promote economic growth and stability. However, the rise of fascism in Europe posed a significant threat to Swedish democracy and the country's political stability.

The rise of fascism in Europe was marked by the emergence of authoritarian regimes in Italy, Germany, and other countries. These regimes were characterized by a commitment to nationalism, militarism, and the suppression of political opposition.

In Sweden, the rise of fascism was met with significant resistance from the country's political and social elites. The Swedish government sought to promote democratic ideals and resist the spread of fascism, even as it faced pressure from far-right movements and other extremist groups.

Despite these challenges, Sweden was able to maintain its democratic traditions and resist the rise of fascism throughout the interwar period. The country's commitment to democracy and social welfare helped to establish

Sweden as a leader in the global progressive movement, and it helped to shape the country's political and cultural identity for decades to come.

In conclusion, the interwar period was a significant period in Swedish history, marked by significant political and economic changes. The rise of fascism in Europe posed a significant threat to Swedish democracy and political stability, but the country was able to resist these pressures and maintain its commitment to democratic ideals and social welfare. Sweden's experience during the interwar period helped to shape the country's political and cultural identity and set the stage for its continued commitment to progressive values and democracy in the decades to come.

Sweden in World War II

Sweden's position of neutrality during World War II was a significant period in Swedish history, marked by political and economic challenges as the country sought to maintain its independence and protect its interests in the face of global conflict.

Sweden declared its neutrality at the beginning of World War II, seeking to avoid involvement in the conflict while protecting its national interests. The country faced significant economic pressures, however, as both the Allied and Axis powers sought to secure Sweden's resources and strategic advantages.

The country's neutrality was also challenged by the rise of Nazi Germany and its aggressive expansionism. Sweden's close proximity to Germany and its strong economic ties with the country made it vulnerable to pressure from the Nazi regime.

Despite these challenges, Sweden was able to maintain its position of neutrality throughout World War II. The country's neutrality was based on a commitment to diplomatic engagement and negotiation, and it sought to avoid direct confrontation with the Axis powers while also resisting pressure from Nazi Germany.

Sweden played an important role in humanitarian efforts during the war, providing aid and support to refugees and other victims of the conflict. The country also played a key role in diplomacy and negotiations, working to promote peace and stability in Europe in the aftermath of the war.

Sweden's position of neutrality during World War II helped to establish the country as a leader in international diplomacy and humanitarian efforts. The country's commitment to social welfare and democratic values also helped to shape the country's political and cultural identity in the aftermath of the conflict.

In conclusion, Sweden's position of neutrality during World War II was a significant period in Swedish history, marked by political and economic challenges as the country sought to maintain its independence and protect its interests in the face of global conflict. Despite these challenges, Sweden was able to maintain its position of neutrality throughout the war and played an important role in humanitarian efforts and international diplomacy. Sweden's experience during World War II helped to shape the country's political and cultural identity and set the stage for its continued commitment to social welfare and democratic values in the decades to come.

The Post-War Social Democratic Consensus

The post-war period in Sweden was marked by significant political, social, and economic changes. The country's commitment to social welfare and democratic values helped to establish a broad consensus among political elites and the public, known as the Social Democratic Consensus.

The Social Democratic Consensus was based on a commitment to social welfare policies, including universal healthcare, education, and housing. The country's commitment to these policies helped to establish Sweden as a leader in the global progressive movement, and it helped to shape the country's political and cultural identity for decades to come.

The post-war period was also marked by significant economic growth and development. Sweden's industrial base expanded rapidly, and the country became a leader in a range of industries, including engineering, telecommunications, and pharmaceuticals. This economic growth was accompanied by significant improvements in living standards and a reduction in poverty and inequality.

The Social Democratic Consensus was challenged by a range of political and economic pressures, including the rise of conservative and neoliberal politics in the 1980s and 1990s. However, the consensus remained a central feature of Swedish politics and society, and it continues to shape the country's political and cultural identity today.

In recent years, the Social Democratic Consensus has come under pressure from changing economic and demographic trends, including globalization and immigration. However, Sweden remains committed to social welfare policies and democratic values, and the Social Democratic Consensus continues to play an important role in shaping the country's political and cultural identity.

In conclusion, the post-war period in Sweden was marked by significant political, social, and economic changes. The country's commitment to social welfare policies and democratic values helped to establish a broad consensus among political elites and the public, known as the Social Democratic Consensus. Despite challenges in recent years, the consensus continues to shape Sweden's political and cultural identity and remains an important feature of the country's political landscape.

The Swedish Model of Welfare

The Swedish Model of Welfare is a social welfare system that has been developed over many decades and has become a defining feature of Sweden's political and cultural identity. It is based on the principles of universalism, social solidarity, and democratic participation.

The Swedish Model of Welfare provides a wide range of social benefits and services to citizens, including healthcare, education, child care, and elderly care. These benefits are available to all citizens and are funded through a combination of taxes and government subsidies.

One of the key features of the Swedish Model of Welfare is its commitment to universalism. This means that social benefits are available to all citizens, regardless of income, employment status, or other factors. This ensures that all citizens have access to basic social services and helps to reduce inequality and poverty.

Another important feature of the Swedish Model of Welfare is its emphasis on social solidarity. This means that the welfare system is designed to promote a sense of collective responsibility and mutual support among citizens. This helps to foster a strong sense of community and social cohesion.

The Swedish Model of Welfare is also characterized by a high degree of democratic participation. Citizens have a strong voice in shaping social policy through democratic institutions, such as political parties, labor unions, and other interest groups. This helps to ensure that social policy is responsive to the needs and concerns of citizens.

The Swedish Model of Welfare has been subject to criticism and debate in recent years, particularly in the context of changing economic and demographic trends. Some critics argue that the welfare system is unsustainable and that it has led to high taxes and reduced economic competitiveness. Others argue that the system is too centralized and bureaucratic, and that it does not provide enough choice or flexibility to citizens.

Despite these criticisms, the Swedish Model of Welfare remains a central feature of Sweden's political and cultural identity. It has helped to establish the country as a leader in the global progressive movement and has played an important role in shaping the country's political and economic development over the past century.

In conclusion, the Swedish Model of Welfare is a social welfare system that is based on the principles of universalism, social solidarity, and democratic participation. It provides a wide range of social benefits and services to citizens and helps to reduce inequality and poverty. While the system has been subject to criticism and debate, it remains a central feature of Sweden's political and cultural identity and continues to play an important role in shaping the country's future.

The 1968 Movement and its Impact on Swedish Society

The 1968 movement was a social and political movement that emerged in Sweden and other parts of the world in the late 1960s. The movement was characterized by a range of social and political demands, including greater political participation, greater personal freedom, and greater social equality.

The 1968 movement in Sweden was closely linked to the country's broader social and political context. At the time, Sweden was experiencing rapid social change and economic growth, which was accompanied by significant social and cultural upheaval.

The movement was particularly influential among young people, who were drawn to its anti-authoritarian ethos and its emphasis on personal freedom and social equality. The movement also had a significant impact on Swedish politics and society, and it helped to shape the country's political and cultural identity in important ways.

One of the key impacts of the 1968 movement on Swedish society was its emphasis on social equality and personal freedom. The movement helped to raise awareness of a range of social issues, including gender inequality, racism, and environmental degradation. It also helped to inspire a range of social reforms, including greater rights for women, greater environmental protections, and greater support for minority groups.

The 1968 movement also had a significant impact on Swedish politics. It helped to inspire the emergence of new political parties and social movements, including the Left Party and the Green Party. It also helped to shift the political agenda in Sweden, with a greater emphasis on social equality and personal freedom.

However, the 1968 movement was also subject to criticism and debate. Some critics argued that the movement was too radical and that its demands were unrealistic or utopian. Others argued that the movement was too focused on individual freedom and not enough on collective responsibility or social cohesion.

Despite these criticisms, the 1968 movement remains an important and influential part of Swedish history. It helped to shape the country's political and cultural identity in important ways and remains a source of inspiration for many activists and social movements today.

In conclusion, the 1968 movement was a social and political movement that emerged in Sweden and other parts of the world in the late 1960s. It had a significant impact on Swedish society, inspiring greater social equality and personal freedom. The movement also helped to shift the political agenda in Sweden and remains an important and influential part of the country's history.

Sweden's Foreign Policy during the Cold War

Sweden's foreign policy during the Cold War was marked by its policy of neutrality and non-alignment. This policy was shaped by a range of factors, including Sweden's geopolitical position, its history of neutrality, and its commitment to democratic values and human rights.

Sweden's policy of neutrality was established in the aftermath of World War II, when the country sought to maintain its independence and avoid becoming embroiled in the global conflicts of the Cold War era. The country remained officially neutral throughout the Cold War, refusing to align itself with either the Western or Soviet blocs.

Despite its policy of neutrality, Sweden remained active in international affairs during the Cold War era. The country played an important role in the establishment of the United Nations and was a leading voice in international efforts to promote disarmament, human rights, and environmental protection.

Sweden's foreign policy during the Cold War was also shaped by its relationship with the Soviet Union. While Sweden maintained a policy of neutrality, it also maintained diplomatic and economic ties with the Soviet Union, and the two countries engaged in a range of cultural and scientific exchanges.

At the same time, Sweden also maintained close ties with the Western powers, particularly the United States. The country participated in a range of military and economic alliances with the West, including the European Free Trade Association and the Non-Aligned Movement.

One of the key challenges facing Sweden's foreign policy during the Cold War was its relationship with neighboring countries, particularly Norway and Denmark. These countries were members of NATO and had close ties with the United States, which put pressure on Sweden to align itself more closely with the West.

Despite these challenges, Sweden remained committed to its policy of neutrality and non-alignment throughout the Cold War era. This policy helped to shape the country's international reputation as a responsible and principled actor in global affairs, and it remains an important part of Sweden's identity and foreign policy today.

In conclusion, Sweden's foreign policy during the Cold War was marked by its policy of neutrality and non-alignment. The country played an active role in international affairs, promoting disarmament, human rights, and environmental protection. While Sweden maintained diplomatic and economic ties with both the Soviet Union and the West, it remained committed to its policy of neutrality, which helped to shape the country's international reputation and identity.

The Assassination of Olof Palme

The assassination of Olof Palme, Sweden's Prime Minister, on February 28, 1986, was a shocking event that stunned the country and sent shockwaves around the world. Palme was one of Sweden's most beloved and charismatic politicians, known for his progressive politics and his commitment to social justice and human rights.

The assassination took place on a busy street in central Stockholm, as Palme and his wife were walking home from a cinema. The attacker approached the couple and shot Palme in the back before fleeing the scene. Palme's wife was also injured in the attack but survived.

The murder of Palme sent shockwaves throughout Sweden and the world. The killer was never caught, despite one of the largest manhunts in Swedish history. The assassination remains one of Sweden's most enduring mysteries, and there are many theories and speculations about who was responsible for the crime.

In the aftermath of the assassination, Sweden was thrown into a state of shock and mourning. Thousands of people took to the streets to express their grief and anger, and the country's political landscape was forever changed.

Palme's death was a profound loss for Sweden and for the international community. He was a key figure in the global fight against apartheid, and his commitment to social justice and human rights inspired people around the world.

In conclusion, the assassination of Olof Palme was a shocking and tragic event that had a profound impact on Sweden and the international community. Palme was a beloved and charismatic politician who inspired people around the world with his commitment to social justice and human rights. The fact that his killer has never been found has only added to the sense of mystery and intrigue surrounding the case, and it remains one of Sweden's most enduring mysteries.

Sweden in the European Union

Sweden joined the European Union (EU) on January 1, 1995, after a referendum in November 1994. The decision to join the EU was a controversial one, with a deeply divided population and political class.

Sweden's decision to join the EU was based on several factors, including the desire to participate in the single market, the hope for greater international cooperation, and the belief that membership would enhance Sweden's political influence in Europe and the world.

Since joining the EU, Sweden has become a prominent member of the bloc. Sweden has been a strong supporter of the EU's enlargement policy, which has seen the EU expand from 15 member states to 27 member states. Sweden has also been a strong advocate of the EU's efforts to promote economic growth, social justice, and environmental protection.

Sweden has also been an active participant in the EU's foreign policy, and has played a key role in shaping the EU's response to global challenges such as climate change, migration, and international security.

Sweden has, however, maintained a cautious approach to the EU's integration process. Sweden has opted out of the Eurozone, choosing to retain its own currency, the Swedish krona. Sweden has also opted out of several EU policies, including the Common Agriculture Policy and the Common Security and Defense Policy.

Sweden's position on EU membership remains complex and evolving. While there is broad public support for Sweden's membership in the EU, there is also a strong strain of Euroscepticism within Swedish politics and society. Some argue that the EU represents a threat to Swedish sovereignty and national identity, while others believe that the EU's focus on market liberalization and deregulation is incompatible with Sweden's social democratic traditions.

Despite these debates and tensions, Sweden remains a committed and active member of the EU. Sweden's membership in the EU has brought numerous benefits, including increased trade and investment opportunities, greater political influence, and closer cooperation with other EU member states.

In conclusion, Sweden's membership in the European Union has been a complex and evolving issue since its accession in 1995. While there is broad public support for membership, there is also a strong strain of Euroscepticism within Swedish politics and society. Despite these debates and tensions, Sweden remains a committed and active member of the EU, with a key role in shaping the bloc's policies and priorities.

Contemporary Politics and Society

Contemporary Sweden is a highly developed and prosperous country with a thriving social democracy, a strong economy, and a reputation for social and environmental responsibility. The country has undergone significant social and political changes in recent years, including a rise in immigration, increasing inequality, and a growing sense of political polarization.

The current political system in Sweden is a parliamentary democracy, with a constitutional monarchy as the head of state. The government is composed of a prime minister and cabinet, and the unicameral parliament, known as the Riksdag, is composed of 349 members elected every four years through a proportional representation system.

The Social Democratic Party has been the dominant political force in Sweden for much of the post-war period, and has formed the government for most of that time. However, in recent years, Sweden has seen a shift towards political fragmentation and polarization, with the rise of new political parties and movements on both the left and right of the political spectrum.

Immigration has been a major issue in Swedish politics in recent years. Sweden has traditionally been a welcoming country for refugees and immigrants, but the country's generous asylum policy has come under strain in the face of a large influx of refugees and asylum seekers in the wake of the Syrian civil war. The issue has become highly politicized, with some parties calling for stricter immigration controls and others advocating for continued openness and tolerance.

Sweden is also grappling with increasing levels of inequality, despite its reputation for social equality and welfare policies. The country has one of the highest levels of income inequality among OECD countries, and a growing gap between the wealthy and the rest of the population. This has led to calls for greater taxation of the wealthy, as well as a more progressive approach to social policies.

The environment is another key issue in Swedish politics and society. Sweden is one of the world's most environmentally conscious countries, with ambitious targets for reducing carbon emissions and transitioning to a green economy. The country has invested heavily in renewable energy, and has set a goal of becoming carbon neutral by 2045.

In conclusion, contemporary Sweden is a dynamic and rapidly changing country, with a vibrant democracy, a strong economy, and a commitment to social and environmental responsibility. While the country faces challenges, including rising inequality and political polarization, it remains a leader in progressive social policies and environmental sustainability. The future of Sweden will depend on its ability to navigate these challenges and continue to build a society that is inclusive, equitable, and environmentally sustainable.

Swedish Art and Culture

Sweden has a rich and diverse cultural heritage that reflects the country's long and storied history. From the prehistoric rock carvings of the Bronze Age to the contemporary art and music scenes of today, Swedish culture has evolved and adapted over the centuries to reflect the changing social, political, and economic conditions of the country.

Swedish art has a strong tradition of realism and naturalism, with a focus on everyday life and the natural world. The country's art history dates back to the Viking Age, with intricate metalwork and woodcarving representing some of the earliest examples of Swedish artistic expression. In the Middle Ages, Swedish art was heavily influenced by Christian iconography, with elaborate church frescoes and altarpieces dominating the artistic landscape.

During the Renaissance and Baroque periods, Swedish art saw an influx of European influences, with painters and sculptors incorporating classical themes and techniques into their work. The 19th century saw a renewed interest in Swedish national identity, with artists such as Carl Larsson and Anders Zorn depicting rural life and folk traditions in their paintings.

In the 20th century, Swedish art became increasingly diverse and experimental, with artists exploring a wide range of styles and techniques. The influential art movement known as "Nordic modernism" emerged in the 1920s and 30s, with artists such as Gunnar Asplund and Sigurd Lewerentz embracing functionalism and minimalism in their architecture and design work.

Swedish culture is also renowned for its literature, with many acclaimed writers and poets hailing from the country. The 19th century saw the emergence of the "proletarian literature" movement, with writers such as August Strindberg and Selma Lagerlöf exploring themes of social justice and political reform in their work. The mid-20th century saw the rise of a new generation of writers, including Astrid Lindgren and Tove Jansson, whose works for children and young adults have achieved global fame.

In addition to literature and visual arts, Sweden has a thriving music scene that encompasses a wide range of styles and genres. Classical music has a long tradition in the country, with the Royal Stockholm Philharmonic Orchestra and the Royal Swedish Opera among the most prestigious cultural institutions in the country. Sweden is also known for its contributions to popular music, with acts such as ABBA, Roxette, and Ace of Base achieving global success.

Swedish culture is deeply intertwined with the country's social and political history, with many cultural movements and works reflecting the changing attitudes and values of Swedish society. Today, Swedish art and culture continue to evolve and adapt to changing circumstances, reflecting the country's ongoing commitment to innovation and creativity.

Conclusion and Reflections on Sweden's History

Sweden's history is a complex and fascinating story that spans thousands of years. From the Stone Age to the present day, the country has undergone a series of political, social, and cultural transformations that have shaped its identity and its place in the world.

One of the most striking features of Sweden's history is its long tradition of social democracy and welfare state policies. The country's commitment to equality and fairness has earned it a reputation as one of the most egalitarian societies in the world, with a strong emphasis on universal healthcare, education, and social services.

Another defining aspect of Swedish history is the country's long tradition of neutrality in international affairs. From the 19th century through the Cold War era and beyond, Sweden has maintained a policy of non-alignment and non-intervention in foreign conflicts, earning it a reputation as a mediator and peace broker on the world stage.

Sweden's history is also marked by its long tradition of innovation and entrepreneurship. From the Viking Age to the present day, Swedes have been at the forefront of technological and scientific advances, with notable contributions in fields such as engineering, medicine, and computer science.

However, Sweden's history is not without its darker moments. The country's involvement in the slave trade and colonialism, as well as its treatment of the indigenous Sami population, are stains on its history that cannot be ignored or overlooked.

Looking to the future, Sweden faces a number of challenges and opportunities as it continues to navigate a rapidly changing global landscape. Climate change, immigration, and demographic shifts are just a few of the issues that will shape the country's future, while its commitment to innovation and social justice will continue to define its identity and its place in the world.

Overall, Sweden's history is a testament to the resilience and adaptability of its people, as well as their unwavering commitment to social justice and equality. As the country moves forward, it will be important to build on these strengths while addressing the challenges and injustices of the past in order to create a better future for all Swedes.

Thank you for taking the time to read this book on the history of Sweden. We hope you found it informative and engaging, and that it deepened your understanding of this fascinating country and its people.

As a writer, nothing is more rewarding than knowing that your work has made a difference, and we would be honored if you would take a moment to leave a positive review of this book. Your feedback helps us improve our writing and reach a wider audience, and it also helps other readers decide whether or not to pick up this book.

Once again, thank you for your time and for your interest in the history of Sweden. We hope you enjoyed reading this book as much as we enjoyed writing it.

Printed in Great Britain
by Amazon